JESUS LOVES YOU

© Copyright 2025 – All rights reserved
No part of this workbook may be reproduced, duplicated, or transmitted in any form or by any means without the prior written permission of the author or publisher.

Disclaimer Notice:
Every effort has been made to ensure the accuracy and integrity of the content provided. However, no guarantees of any kind are declared or implied.

Sources:
All Bible-derived content is drawn from the NIV, NLT, NASB, and NKJV translations.

Image Notice:
The cover image was created using AI technology and is for illustrative purposes only. All images in this book are symbolic and not meant to represent actual appearance. The images should not be taken as exact representations of products, services, or individuals, and no actual resemblance to any specific person or entity is intended or implied.

Contact Us:

MyBibleWorkbooks@gmail.com

Projectkingdomcome

Projectkingdomcome

PROJECT KINGDOM COME
ISBN 978-1-961786-04-2

Get The Entire Workbook Series!

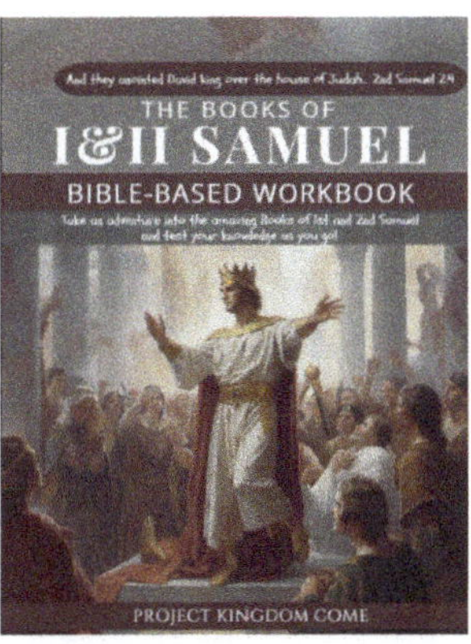

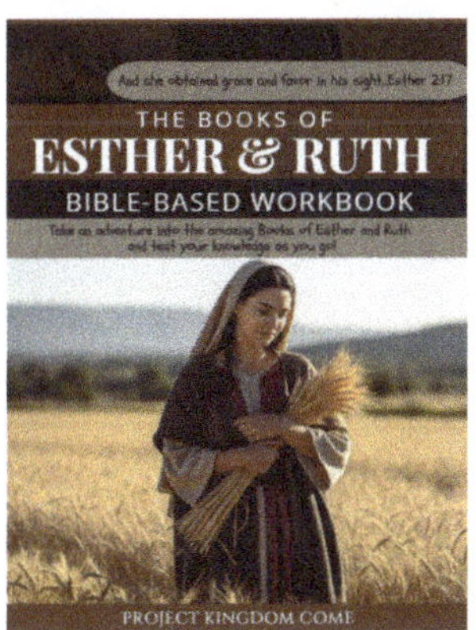

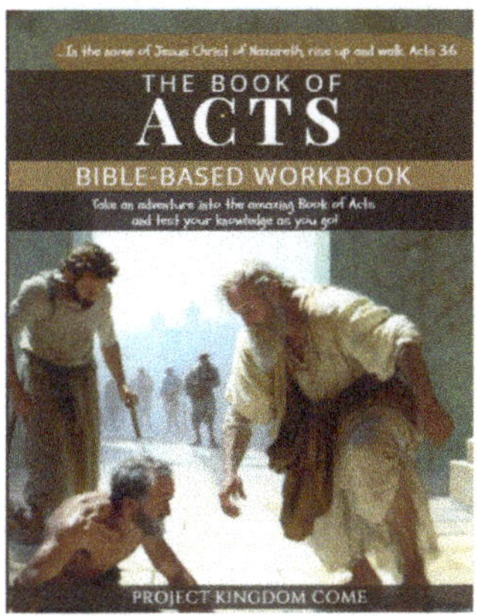

WWW.MYBIBLEWORKBOOKS.COM

This workbook belongs to:

Leave your mark!

HOW TO USE THIS WORKBOOK

This workbook is designed to help young people explore the treasures in God's Word while having fun, growing in faith, and learning how to search the Scriptures for life's answers.

Here is what you will find inside:

Multiple Choice Questions	Each question comes directly from Scripture and includes a reference verse to help with locating the answer in the Bible. If possible, use a physical Bible to search for the answers.
Weekly Segments	Questions are grouped in weekly categories that could also be completed in a shorter or longer time frame.
Weekly Memory Verses	At the start of every week is a Bible verse to memorize. Each day of that week will repeat that memory verse with a chance to test memorization at the end of the week.
Certificate of Completion	At the end of the workbook, please find a Certificate of Achievement, ready for the child's name and parent or teacher's signature. Celebrate the accomplishment of studying an entire book in the Bible!
Answer Key	The workbook contains an answer key to serve as a support tool for parents or teachers reviewing the responses.

Recommendation for Parents and/or Teachers: Review the responses with your child or student and discuss lessons learned or interesting insights, to improve the child's retention and enrichment in the knowledge of God's word.

You can do all things through Christ who gives you strength!
Philippians 4:13

SAMPLE QUESTION...

HOW TO USE THIS WORKBOOK

Reading the reference verse will always lead you to the correct answer!

In the beginning, God created: (Genesis 1:1)

(A) The Heavens and the Earth
B. Heaven and Earth
C. Heaven only
D. Earth only

The number that comes after the book is the 'Chapter'

This is the name of a book in the Bible

Joshua 1:8

The number after the chapter is the 'Verse'

NOW TEST YOURSELF! FIND JOSHUA CHAPTER 1 VERSE 8 IN YOUR BIBLE!

INTRODUCTION: THE BOOK OF ESTHER

For Such a Time as This

The Book of **Esther** is a story of courage, purpose, and **divine timing**. Even though God's name is never mentioned in this book, we see His hand at work in every chapter — arranging events, protecting His people, and using an ordinary girl to do something extraordinary.

Esther was chosen to be queen, but God had a **greater plan** for her life — to help save her people from danger. She had to be brave, wise, and trust that **God was with her** even when things were scary.

As you study Esther, you will discover:

- **God places us exactly where we need to be**
- **Courage is doing the right thing, even when it's hard**
- **God can use anyone to accomplish His plan**
- **You were created for a purpose — on purpose!**

Esther teaches us that we don't have to be loud or famous to make a difference. All we need is a willing heart, and God will do the rest — because we are all here for such a time as this!

"And who knows whether you have come to the kingdom for such a time as this?"
Esther 4:14

WEEK 1

1. How many provinces from India to Ethiopia did King Ahasuerus rule? (Esther 1:1)

A. 7
B. 27
C. 127
D. 128

2. For how many days did the feast King Ahasuerus prepared for his officials and servants last? (Esther 1:3-4)

A. 120 days
B. 150 days
C. 180 days
D. 200 days

WEEK 1 MEMORY VERSE: PROVERBS 21:1

The King's heart is in the hand of the LORD, like the rivers of water; He turns it wherever He wishes.

WEEK 1

3. What did the King ask Queen Vashti to do? (Esther 1:10-11)

A. Appear before him wearing her royal crown to display her beauty before the people and officials
B. Greet the guests with a speech
C. Prepare a feast for the women
D. Lead a royal procession

4. Who did King Ahasuerus speak to about Queen Vashti's refusal to come before him? (Esther 1:13-15)

A. His personal advisors
B. The elders of the city
C. The seven princes of Persia and Media
D. His counselors from the court

WEEK 1 MEMORY VERSE: PROVERBS 21:1

The King's heart is in the hand of the LORD, like the rivers of water; He turns it wherever He wishes.

WEEK 1

5. What did Memucan warn would happen if Vashti's actions went unaddressed? (Esther 1:16-18)

A. All the women would dishonor their husbands
B. The noblemen would lose authority
C. Both A and B
D. The king would appear weak

6. What did Memucan advise the king to do about Queen Vashti? (Esther 1:19)

A. Send her into exile in a distant land
B. Issue a royal decree that she may never again appear before the king
C. Appoint a new queen more worthy than her
D. Both B and C

WEEK 1 MEMORY VERSE: PROVERBS 21:1

The King's heart is in the hand of the LORD, like the rivers of water; He turns it wherever He wishes.

WEEK 1

7. Why did the king agree to remove Queen Vashti from her royal position? (Esther 1:20)

A. To set an example so all wives would honor their husbands
B. To punish Vashti for her boldness
C. Because he had found someone else
D. None of the above

8. How was the next queen to be chosen? (Esther 2:1-4)

A. Officers were appointed to gather beautiful young virgins
B. The virgins would be placed under the care of Hegai
C. The king would choose one to become queen
D. All the above

WEEK 1 MEMORY VERSE: PROVERBS 21:1

The King's heart is in the hand of the LORD, like the rivers of water; He turns it wherever He wishes.

WEEK 1

9. Who is Hadassah? (Esther 2:7)

A. A Hebrew servant
B. Esther
C. A friend of Mordecai
D. Esther's friend

10. How was Mordecai related to Esther? (Esther 2:7)

A. He was her cousin who raised her like his own daughter
B. He was her father
C. He was her teacher
D. He was her uncle

WEEK 1 MEMORY VERSE: PROVERBS 21:1

The King's heart is in the hand of the LORD, like the rivers of water; He turns it wherever He wishes.

WEEK 1

11. How was Esther treated by Hegai, the custodian of the women? (Esther 2:9)

A. He gave her beauty treatments and special food
B. He assigned seven maidservants to her from the palace
C. He moved her to the best place in the women's quarters
D. All the above

12. What secret was Esther keeping? (Esther 2:10)

A. That her parents had died
B. That she was not from Shushan
C. That she was a Jew and had not revealed her family background
D. That she had been trained as a servant girl

WEEK 1 MEMORY VERSE: PROVERBS 21:1

The King's heart is in the hand of the LORD, like the rivers of water; He turns it wherever He wishes.

WEEK 1

13. How long did the preparation of the young women last before they went before the king? (Esther 2:12)

A. 6 months
B. 9 months
C. 12 months
D. 18 months

14. What were the young women allowed to take with them when they went to see the king? (Esther 2:13)

A. Whatever they desired
B. Whatever the king commanded
C. What their families sent
D. Only perfumes and ornaments

WEEK 1 MEMORY VERSE: PROVERBS 21:1

The King's heart is in the hand of the LORD, like the rivers of water; He turns it wherever He wishes.

KEEP GOING, YOU'RE DOING GREAT!

Even when I feel weak, God is the strength of my heart and my portion forever. I will not be shaken.
(Psalm 73:26)

Great job completing the week!

Did you memorize the daily verse?
Test yourself by writing it here...

Use this space to draw a scene from the Bible or reflect on something you learned, felt or experienced...

WEEK 2

15. Who was Esther's father? (Esther 2:15)

A. Mordecai
B. Abihail
C. Haman
D. The Bible doesn't say

16. When it was Esther's turn to go to the King, what did she request to take with her to the King's palace? (Esther 2:15)

A. Only what Hegai advised
B. What her uncle gave her
C. She didn't take anything
D. Clothes, beauty treatments, and food

WEEK 2 MEMORY VERSE: PSALM 5:12

For You, O Lord, will bless the righteous; with favor you will surround him as with a shield.

WEEK 2

17. Whom did King Ahasuerus make Queen instead of Vashti? (Esther2:17)

A. Ruth
B. Sarah
C. Hannah
D. Esther

18. What plan did Mordecai uncover about Bigthan and Teresh? (Esther 2:21)

A. They plotted to assassinate the king
B. They planned to poison Esther in the palace
C. They intended to steal treasures from the royal treasury
D. They conspired to escape the king's service

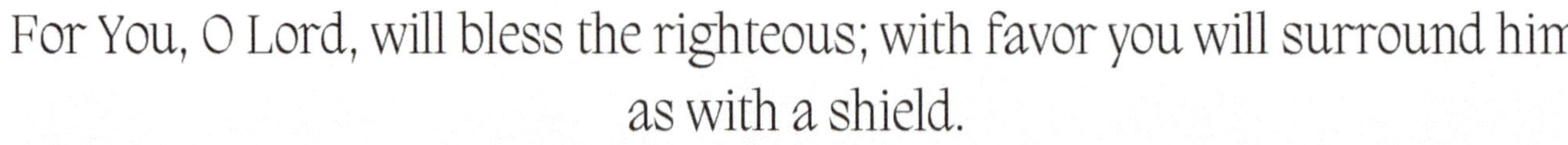

WEEK 2 MEMORY VERSE: PSALM 5:12

For You, O Lord, will bless the righteous; with favor you will surround him as with a shield.

19. What happened after Mordecai exposed the plot against the king? (Esther 2:22-23)

A. He told Esther, who informed the king
B. Bigthan and Teresh were hanged
C. The event was recorded in the royal chronicles
D. All the above

20. What was the man's name whom the King promoted above all the other princes? (Esther 3:1)

A. Mordecai
B. Abihail
C. Hegai
D. Haman

For You, O Lord, will bless the righteous; with favor you will surround him as with a shield.

WEEK 2

21. What did Mordecai refuse to do for Haman? (Esther 3:2)

A. Call him master
B. Bow down and show honor
C. Give him a royal gift
D. Speak well of him to the king

22. Why did Mordecai refuse to bow to Haman? (Esther 3:4)

A. He was a Jew and worshiped only God
B. He disagreed with Haman's leadership
C. He was angry with the king
D. He didn't understand the command

WEEK 2 MEMORY VERSE: PSALM 5:12

For You, O Lord, will bless the righteous; with favor you will surround him as with a shield.

WEEK 2

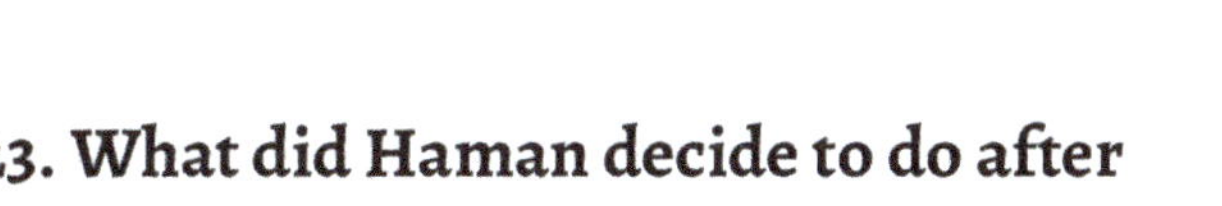

23. What did Haman decide to do after Mordecai refused to honor him? (Esther 3:5-6)

A. Ask the king to remove Mordecai

B. Plan revenge against Mordecai & his family

C. Plot to destroy all Jews in the kingdom

D. Write an accusation against Mordecai to the king

24. What reasons did Haman give the king to justify destroying the Jews? (Esther 3:8-9)

A. They are different and disobey the king's laws

B. The king shouldn't tolerate them

C. Haman offered silver for their destruction

D. All the above

WEEK 2 MEMORY VERSE: PSALM 5:12

For You, O Lord, will bless the righteous; with favor you will surround him as with a shield.

WEEK 2

25. What did the king command his royal secretaries to do? (Esther 3:12-13)

A. Write letters in every language with Haman's orders

B. Order the destruction of all Jews and the seizure of their property

C. Name a date to carry out the destruction

D. All the above

26. What happened in the city of Shushan after the king's decree was announced? (Esther 3:15)

A. The city was thrown into confusion

B. The people protested the king's command

C. The people mourned in the streets

D. The people gathered to pray

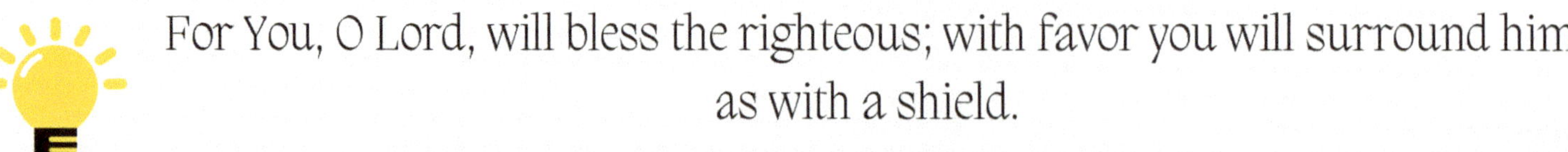

WEEK 2 MEMORY VERSE: PSALM 5:12

For You, O Lord, will bless the righteous; with favor you will surround him as with a shield.

WEEK 2

27. What did Mordecai do when he learned of the king's command? (Esther 4:1-8)

A. Wore sackcloth and ashes and cried out in the city
B. Sent a message and copy of the decree to Esther
C. Asked Esther to plead with the king
D. All the above

28. What was Esther's initial reaction to Mordecai's request that she go to the king? (Esther 4:10-11)

A. She feared death, since it was illegal to approach the king uninvited
B. She boldly agreed to go at once
C. She planned to flee the palace
D. She sent a servant to go instead

WEEK 2 MEMORY VERSE: PSALM 5:12

For You, O Lord, will bless the righteous; with favor you will surround him as with a shield.

Like Esther, I obtain favor
in the sight of all who
see me
(Esther 2:15)

Great job completing the week!

Did you memorize the daily verse?
Test yourself by writing it here...

Use this space to draw a scene from the Bible or reflect on something you learned, felt or experienced...

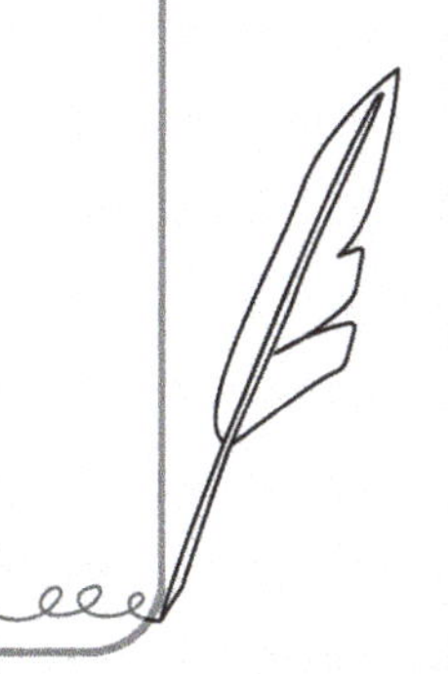

WEEK 3

29. What message did Mordecai send to Esther after she hesitated? (Esther 4:12-14)

A. Don't think you will escape harm just because you're in the palace

B. Help will come from somewhere else if you stay silent

C. Perhaps you were made queen for such a time as this

D. All the above

30. Why did Esther ask Mordecai to gather the Jews for a fast? (Esther 4:15-16)

A. She knew the king might put her to death

B. She was preparing to intercede for her people

C. She wanted the Lord's favor and courage

D. All the above

WEEK 3 MEMORY VERSE: ESTHER 4:14

For if you remain completely silent at this time, relief and deliverance will arise for the Jews from another place, but you and your father's house will perish. Yet who knows whether you have come to the kingdom for such a time as this?"

WEEK 3

31. What did King Ahasuerus do when he saw Esther standing in the inner court in her royal robes? (Esther 5:1-2)

A. He became angry and turned away
B. He held out his golden scepter and welcomed her
C. He sent a servant to speak on his behalf
D. He asked Haman what to do about her

32. What was Esther's request at her first banquet with the king and Haman? (Esther 5:7-8)

A. That the Jews be protected
B. That the king and Haman join her at another banquet
C. That Haman be exposed
D. That Mordecai be honored

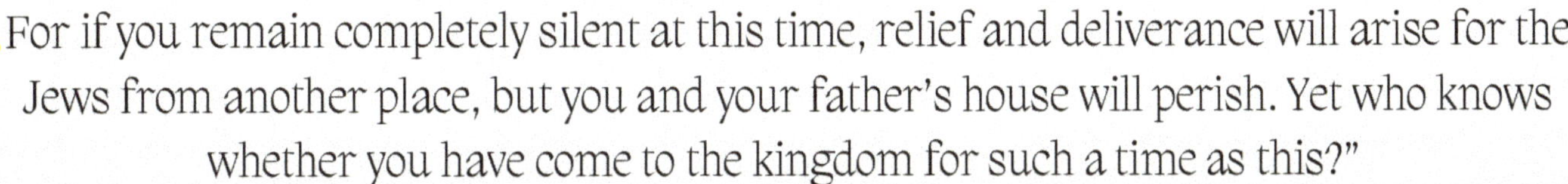

WEEK 3 MEMORY VERSE: ESTHER 4:14

For if you remain completely silent at this time, relief and deliverance will arise for the Jews from another place, but you and your father's house will perish. Yet who knows whether you have come to the kingdom for such a time as this?"

WEEK 3

33. What did Haman boast about to his family and friends? (Esther 5:10-12)

A. His riches and many sons
B. His closeness to the king
C. Being the only one Queen Esther invited
D. All the above

34. Why was Haman still unhappy after the banquet? (Esther 5:13)

A. He wanted more wealth
B. He had not received a reward
C. Mordecai was still sitting at the gate
D. He didn't receive the king's full attention

WEEK 3 MEMORY VERSE: ESTHER 4:14

For if you remain completely silent at this time, relief and deliverance will arise for the Jews from another place, but you and your father's house will perish. Yet who knows whether you have come to the kingdom for such a time as this?"

WEEK 3

35. What did Haman's wife and friends advise him to do about Mordecai? (Esther 5:14)

A. Set up a pole to hang Mordecai
B. Attend the banquet and forget about Mordecai
C. Ask Esther to speak to Mordecai
D. Both A and B

36. What was written in the book of the chronicles about Mordecai? (Esther 6:1-2)

A. That he reported a plot to kill the king
B. That he was related to Queen Esther
C. That he worked at the palace gate
D. That he disobeyed Haman

WEEK 3 MEMORY VERSE: ESTHER 4:14

For if you remain completely silent at this time, relief and deliverance will arise for the Jews from another place, but you and your father's house will perish. Yet who knows whether you have come to the kingdom for such a time as this?"

WEEK 3

37. Why had Haman entered the king's court early that morning? (Esther 6:4)

A. To ask the king about honoring him
B. To tell the king about Esther's feast
C. To request permission to hang Mordecai
D. To discuss palace business

38. Why did Haman describe such elaborate honors to the king? (Esther 6:6-10)

A. He assumed the king was speaking about him
B. He thought he was the most deserving man
C. He wanted to wear the king's robe and ride the king's horse
D. All the above

WEEK 3 MEMORY VERSE: ESTHER 4:14

For if you remain completely silent at this time, relief and deliverance will arise for the Jews from another place, but you and your father's house will perish. Yet who knows whether you have come to the kingdom for such a time as this?"

WEEK 3

39. What warning did Haman's wife and friends give him about Mordecai? (Esther 6:13)

A. You will not win against him, because he is a Jew
B. Mordecai will soon rise in power
C. The queen may protect Mordecai
D. Mordecai will soon be forgotten

40. What happened when Queen Esther hosted her second banquet? (Esther 7:1-10)

A. She revealed Haman's evil plan
B. She asked the king to save her people, the Jews
C. The king ordered Haman to be hanged
D. All the above

WEEK 3 MEMORY VERSE: ESTHER 4:14

For if you remain completely silent at this time, relief and deliverance will arise for the Jews from another place, but you and your father's house will perish. Yet who knows whether you have come to the kingdom for such a time as this?"

WEEK 3

41. What happened on the day Haman was hanged? (Esther 8:1-2)

A. The king gave Esther Haman's house
B. Esther told the king how she was related to Mordecai
C. The king gave Mordecai Haman's signet ring
D. All the above

42. Who did Queen Esther appoint to oversee Haman's estate? (Esther 8:2)

A. Her personal steward
B. Mordecai
C. One of the king's eunuchs
D. A trusted advisor

WEEK 3 MEMORY VERSE: ESTHER 4:14

For if you remain completely silent at this time, relief and deliverance will arise for the Jews from another place, but you and your father's house will perish. Yet who knows whether you have come to the kingdom for such a time as this?"

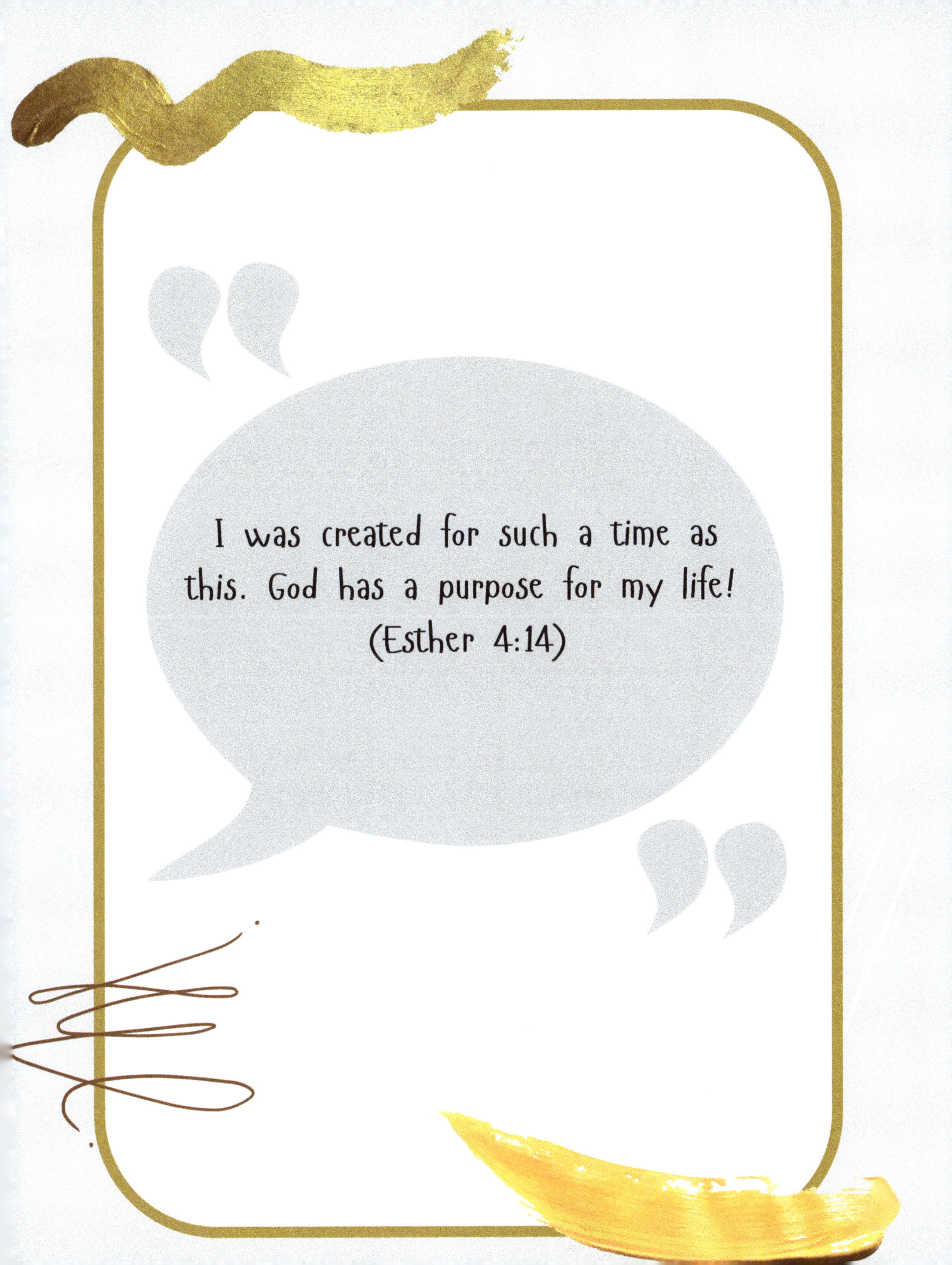
I was created for such a time as this. God has a purpose for my life!
(Esther 4:14)

Great job completing the week!

Did you memorize the daily verse?
Test yourself by writing it here...

Use this space to draw a scene from the Bible or reflect on something you learned, felt or experienced...

WEEK 4

43. What happened after Esther pleaded with the king to reverse Haman's orders? (Esther 8:5-11)

A. The king summoned the royal secretaries
B. Mordecai's new orders were written in every language and province
C. The Jews were allowed to defend themselves and take their enemies' property
D. All the above

44. What did Mordecai's decree allow the Jews to do? (Esther 8:11)

A. Hide from their enemies
B. Run to the palace for protection
C. Defend themselves and destroy anyone who attacked them
D. Escape to another nation

WEEK 4 MEMORY VERSE: PSALM 20:7
Some trust in chariots, and some in horses; but we will remember the name of the Lord our God.

WEEK 4

45. Why did many people of other nationalities decide to become Jews? (Esther 8:17)

A. The fear of the Jews fell upon them
B. They wanted to be favored by Mordecai
C. They were afraid of the king's decree
D. They hoped to escape judgment

46. What else did the Jews do when they killed 500 men in Shushan? (Esther 9:6-10)

A. They took silver and gold
B. They killed Haman's ten sons but took no plunder
C. They captured the palace
D. They honored the king with a parade

WEEK 4 MEMORY VERSE: PSALM 20:7
Some trust in chariots, and some in horses; but we will remember the name of the Lord our God.

WEEK 4

47. What was Esther's request regarding Haman's ten sons? (Esther 9:13)

A. That their bodies be hanged publicly on the pole
B. That their names be erased from history
C. That they be buried with royal honor
D. That they be sent to another province

48. How did the Jews celebrate their victory on the 14th and 15th of Adar? (Esther 9:20-22)

A. With a holy assembly
B. By offering sacrifices
C. By sending gifts to one another and to the poor
D. By fasting and praying

WEEK 4 MEMORY VERSE: PSALM 20:7
Some trust in chariots, and some in horses; but we will remember the name of the Lord our God.

WEEK 4

49. What are the names of the two days the Jews celebrate in Adar? (Esther 9:26-27)

A. Purim
B. Shabbat
C. Hanukkah
D. Yom Kippur

50. Esther is also known as Hadassah (Esther 2:7)

A. True
B. False

WEEK 4 MEMORY VERSE: PSALM 20:7

Some trust in chariots, and some in horses; but we will remember the name of the Lord our God.

WEEK 4

51. Esther was the daughter of Abihail, Mordecai's brother (Esther 2:15)

A. True
B. False

52. Haman was willing to give ten thousand talents of silver to the king's treasury to destroy the Jews (Esther 3:8-10)

A. True
B. False

WEEK 4 MEMORY VERSE: PSALM 20:7

Some trust in chariots, and some in horses; but we will remember the name of the Lord our God.

53. A copy of the order to destroy all Jews was issued as law in every province and made known to all people. (Esther 3:12-14)

A. True
B. False

54 . Purim is a type of food for the Jews (Esther 9:26)

A. True
B. False

WEEK 4 MEMORY VERSE: PSALM 20:7
Some trust in chariots, and some in horses; but we will remember the name of the Lord our God.

WEEK 4

55. An order was written that the celebration of Purim should continue throughout all generations as a reminder for the Jews about how they were delivered from their enemies (Esther 9:20-28)

A. True
B. False

56. Mordecai was promoted and became second in rank to King Ahasuerus (Esther 10:3)

A. True
B. False

WEEK 4 MEMORY VERSE: PSALM 20:7

Some trust in chariots, and some in horses; but we will remember the name of the Lord our God.

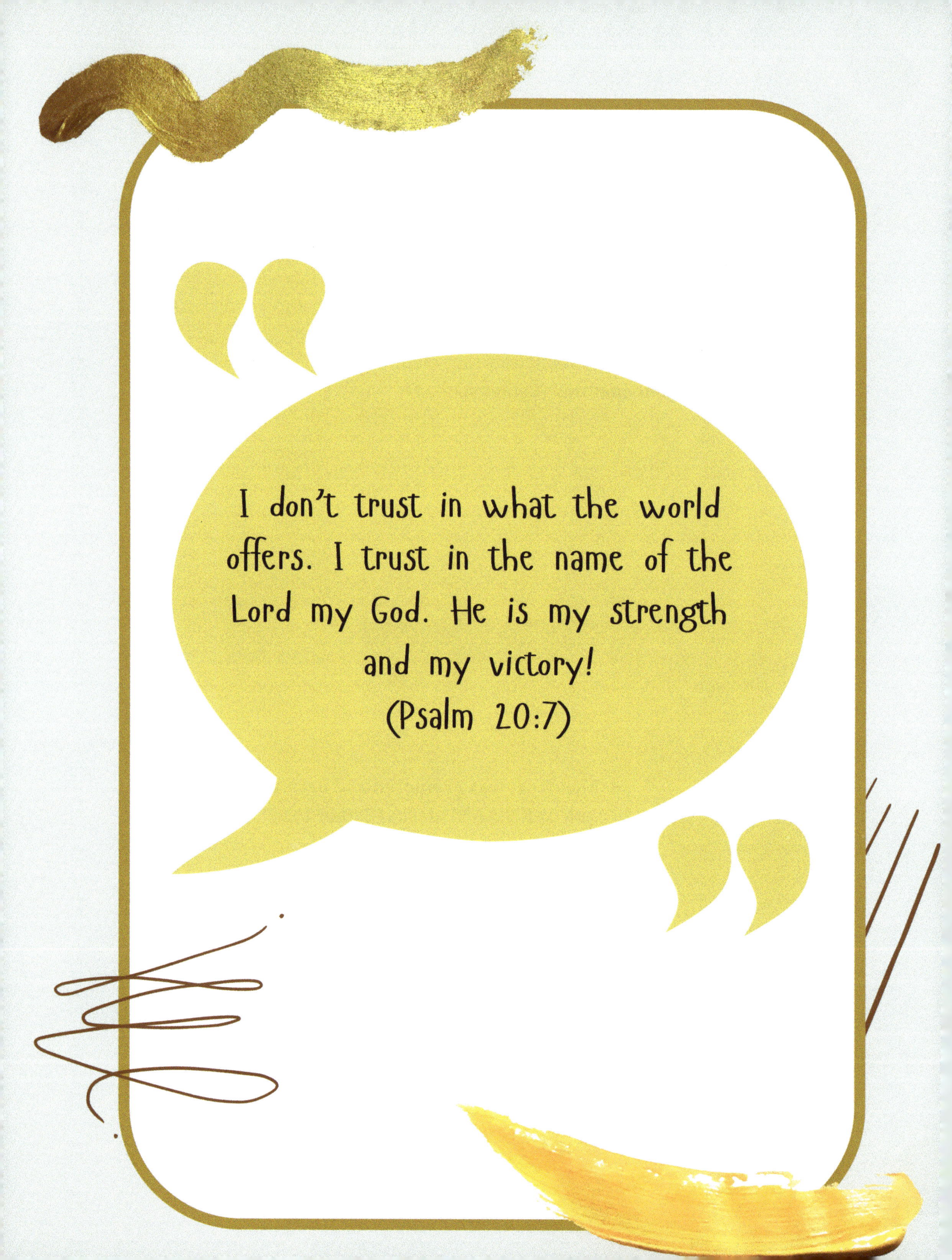
I don't trust in what the world offers. I trust in the name of the Lord my God. He is my strength and my victory!
(Psalm 20:7)

Great job completing the week!

Did you memorize the daily verse?
Test yourself by writing it here...

Use this space to draw a scene from the Bible or reflect on something you learned, felt or experienced...

INTRODUCTION: THE BOOK OF RUTH

A Story of Loyalty, Redemption & God's Perfect Plan

The Book of Ruth is a beautiful reminder that even in seasons of loss and uncertainty, **God is always working behind the scenes**. Ruth was a young woman from Moab who chose to follow the one true God, even when it meant leaving everything behind.

Her story is full of courage, kindness, loyalty, and hope. Even though Ruth started with nothing, God honored her faith and brought her into a brand-new future; one that would lead straight to the family line of **King David**... and later, Jesus!

As you journey through Ruth, you will learn:

- **God sees you, even when life is hard**
- **Your choices of faith and kindness matter**
- **God redeems what seems lost**
- **God's plans are bigger than your beginnings**

This small book carries a big message: **God is always working,** and **you are never forgotten.** Ruth's story proves that when we choose to follow God, He can turn every "why me?" moment into a "look what the Lord has done!" miracle.

"Your people shall be my people, and your God, my God."
Ruth 1:16

WEEK 5

57. The story of Ruth takes place during which period in Israel's history? (Ruth 1:1)

A. When kings ruled over Israel
B. During the days of the prophets
C. When the Judges ruled
D. After the exile to Babylon

58. Why did Elimelech move his family from Bethlehem in Judah to the country of Moab? (Ruth 1:1-2)

A. He was looking for wives for his sons
B. There was a severe famine in Judah
C. He hoped to find better job opportunities
D. He missed his relatives in Moab

WEEK 5 MEMORY VERSE: RUTH 1:6

Entreat me not to leave you, Or to turn back from following after you; For wherever you go, I will go; And wherever you lodge, I will lodge; Your people shall be my people, And your God, my God.

WEEK 5

59. What was the name of Elimelech's wife? (Ruth 1:2)

A. Ruth
B. Naomi
C. Orpah
D. Mary

60. What major events happened while Naomi's family lived in Moab? (Ruth 1:3-6)

A. Naomi's sons married Moabite women
B. Elimelech and both sons died
C. Naomi became wealthy in Moab
D. Both A and B

WEEK 5 MEMORY VERSE: RUTH 1:6

Entreat me not to leave you, Or to turn back from following after you; For wherever you go, I will go; And wherever you lodge, I will lodge; Your people shall be my people, And your God, my God.

WEEK 5

61. Which daughter-in-law refused to leave Naomi and insisted on going with her to Judah? (Ruth 1:14)

A. Ruth
B. Orpah
C. Both Ruth and Orpah
D. Neither of them

62. Why did Naomi encourage her daughters-in-law to return to their families in Moab? (Ruth 1:11-13)

A. She was too old to care for them
B. She didn't want them to follow her
C. She believed they could remarry and have a better future in their homeland
D. She wanted to travel back to Judah alone

WEEK 5 MEMORY VERSE: RUTH 1:6

Entreat me not to leave you, Or to turn back from following after you; For wherever you go, I will go; And wherever you lodge, I will lodge; Your people shall be my people, And your God, my God.

WEEK 5

63. How did Ruth respond to Naomi when she told her to return home? (Ruth 1:16-17)

A. "Wherever you go, I will go. Wherever you stay, I will stay."
B. "Your people will be my people, and your God will be my God."
C. "May the Lord punish me if anything but death separates us."
D. All of the above

64. What new name did Naomi ask the people of Bethlehem to call her? (Ruth 1:20)

A. Maya
B. Mara
C. Mom
D. Ruth, in honor of her daughter-in-law

WEEK 5 MEMORY VERSE: RUTH 1:6

Entreat me not to leave you, Or to turn back from following after you; For wherever you go, I will go; And wherever you lodge, I will lodge; Your people shall be my people, And your God, my God.

WEEK 5

65. Why did Naomi say she should no longer be called Naomi? (Ruth 1:20-21)

A. She felt the Lord had made her life bitter and brought misfortune upon her

B. She didn't want to be reminded of her past

C. She felt ashamed to be back in Bethlehem

D. She was asked to change her name by the town elders

66. When did Naomi and Ruth arrive in Bethlehem? (Ruth 1:22)

A. In the middle of winter

B. During the Feast of Weeks

C. At the beginning of the barley harvest

D. In late spring during Passover

WEEK 5 MEMORY VERSE: RUTH 1:6

Entreat me not to leave you, Or to turn back from following after you; For wherever you go, I will go; And wherever you lodge, I will lodge; Your people shall be my people, And your God, my God.

WEEK 5

67. What was the name of the wealthy man in Bethlehem who was a relative of Elimelech? (Ruth 2:1)

A. Chilion

B. Mahlon

C. Boaz

D. His name was not mentioned

68. Why did the rich man show Ruth kindness when she went to work in his fields? (Ruth 2:8-12)

A. He thought Naomi would make a good match for him

B. He noticed Ruth was beautiful and quiet

C. He had heard how faithful Ruth had been to Naomi

D. He had no other workers available that day

WEEK 5 MEMORY VERSE: RUTH 1:6

Entreat me not to leave you, Or to turn back from following after you; For wherever you go, I will go; And wherever you lodge, I will lodge; Your people shall be my people, And your God, my God.

WEEK 5

69. What had Boaz heard about Ruth that made him admire her? (Ruth 2:11)

A. That she was an excellent cook

B. That she left her homeland and family to care for Naomi among strangers

C. That she worked long hours in the field

D. That she used to be a princess in Moab

70. What did Naomi say to Ruth about Boaz after Ruth returned from the fields? (Ruth 2:20–22)

A. Boaz was a kind and generous man

B. Boaz was a close relative and one of their kinsman-redeemers

C. Boaz might ask Ruth to marry him

D. Boaz had many workers who would protect Ruth

WEEK 5 MEMORY VERSE: RUTH 1:6

Entreat me not to leave you, Or to turn back from following after you; For wherever you go, I will go; And wherever you lodge, I will lodge; Your people shall be my people, And your God, my God.

I choose to follow God. His people are my people, and I belong to Him!
(Ruth 1:16)

Great job completing the week!

Did you memorize the daily verse?
Test yourself by writing it here...

Use this space to draw a scene from the Bible or reflect on something you learned, felt or experienced...

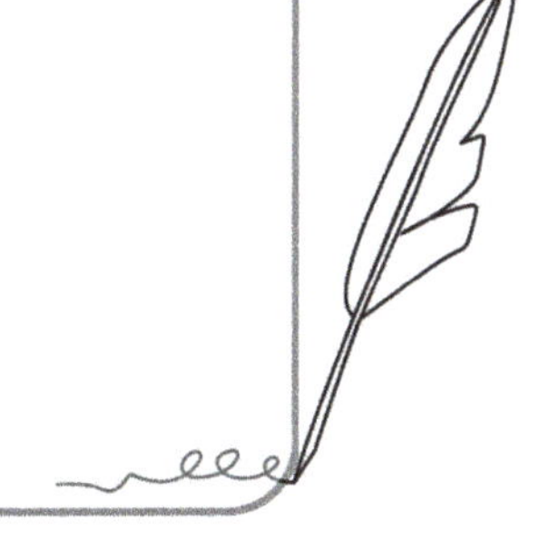

WEEK 6

71. How long did Ruth continue working in Boaz's field (Ruth 2:23)

A. Until the end of the barley and wheat harvests

B. For three weeks

C. Until Naomi asked her to stop

D. For seven years

72. Why did Naomi give Ruth advice about approaching Boaz at the threshing floor? (Ruth 3:1)

A. Naomi was ready for Ruth to leave her home

B. Ruth had become a burden to the household

C. Naomi wanted Ruth to find a godly husband who would care for her

D. Boaz had asked Naomi to help him find a wife

WEEK 6 MEMORY VERSE: RUTH 2:12

The Lord repay your work, and a full reward be given you by the Lord God of Israel, under whose wings you have come for refuge.

WEEK 6

73. Which of the following was NOT part of Naomi's advice to Ruth? (Ruth 3:1–4)

A. Wash and put on your best clothes
B. Wait until Boaz has finished eating and drinking
C. Uncover his feet and lie down
D. Tell Boaz he must marry you immediately

74. When Ruth approached Boaz during the night, what did she say to him? (Ruth 3:9)

A. "I have come to serve you, my lord."
B. "Naomi told me to lie here until you wake up."
C. "I am your servant Ruth. Spread your covering over me, for you are a close relative."
D. Ruth said nothing and quietly walked away

WEEK 6 MEMORY VERSE: RUTH 2:12

The Lord repay your work, and a full reward be given you by the Lord God of Israel, under whose wings you have come for refuge.

WEEK 6

75. How did Boaz respond when he discovered Ruth lying at his feet? (Ruth 3:10–13)

A. He asked her to leave immediately
B. He scolded her for coming at night
C. He praised her for her kindness and promised to redeem her if the closer relative did not
D. He asked Ruth to return with Naomi in the morning

76. What did Boaz give Ruth to take home the next morning? (Ruth 3:15)

A. A ring and necklace
B. Six measures of barley wrapped in her shawl
C. A blanket and water jug
D. A letter for Naomi

WEEK 6 MEMORY VERSE: RUTH 2:12

The Lord repay your work, and a full reward be given you by the Lord God of Israel, under whose wings you have come for refuge.

WEEK 6

77. What did Boaz do the morning after his meeting with Ruth at the threshing floor? (Ruth 4:1–6)

A. He returned to the field and sent Ruth a message
B. He went to the town gate and gathered ten elders to meet with Ruth's closest relative
C. He announced his wedding to Ruth publicly
D. He sent Naomi a gift for her kindness

78. What did Boaz ask the closest relative when they met at the gate? (Ruth 4:3–5)

A. If he would give Ruth money for her labor
B. If he would bless Naomi's household
C. If he was willing to redeem Elimelech's land and marry Ruth
D. If he wanted to hire Ruth to work in his fields again

WEEK 6 MEMORY VERSE: RUTH 2:12

The Lord repay your work, and a full reward be given you by the Lord God of Israel, under whose wings you have come for refuge.

WEEK 6

79. What sign did the closest relative give to Boaz to confirm their agreement? (Ruth 4:7–8)

A. He bowed down to Boaz in front of the elders
B. He gave Boaz a firm handshake
C. He removed his sandal and gave it to Boaz
D. All the above

80. What did it mean for Boaz to "redeem" the land? (Ruth 4:9–10)

A. He was buying the land to build a house
B. He was forgiving Naomi's debt
C. He would buy the land and take Ruth as his wife so her husband's family name would continue
D. He would donate the land back to the tribe of Judah

WEEK 6 MEMORY VERSE: RUTH 2:12

The Lord repay your work, and a full reward be given you by the Lord God of Israel, under whose wings you have come for refuge.

WEEK 6

81. What blessings did the elders and witnesses speak over Boaz and Ruth at the town gate? (Ruth 4:11–12)

A. That Ruth would have many sons
B. That Boaz would be rich and well-known
C. That Boaz would become a judge in Israel
D. That Ruth would be like Rachel and Leah, that Boaz would prosper, and that their house would be like Perez's

82. Who named the baby after Ruth gave birth to a son? (Ruth 4:17)

A. Ruth
B. Boaz
C. Naomi
D. The women of the neighborhood

WEEK 6 MEMORY VERSE: RUTH 2:12

The Lord repay your work, and a full reward be given you by the Lord God of Israel, under whose wings you have come for refuge.

WEEK 6

83. Which of the following statements are true about Ruth's son, Obed? (Ruth 4:17–22)

A. He became the father of Jesse
B. He became the grandfather of David
C. Both A and B
D. He became a farmer in Moab

84. What did the women of Bethlehem say about Ruth to Naomi after the baby was born? (Ruth 4:15)

A. That she would make a great grandmother
B. That Boaz was lucky to have Ruth
C. That Ruth was better to Naomi than seven sons
D. That Ruth's story should be written in the temple

WEEK 6 MEMORY VERSE: RUTH 2:12

The Lord repay your work, and a full reward be given you by the Lord God of Israel, under whose wings you have come for refuge.

I am God's servant, and He takes pleasure in my prosperity
(Psalm 35:27)

Great job completing the week!

Did you memorize the daily verse?
Test yourself by writing it here...

Use this space to draw a scene from the Bible or reflect on something you learned, felt or experienced...

This Certificate Certifies That:

Has Successfully Completed The Esther & Ruth Workbook!

PARENT/TEACHER SIGNATURE

Flo & Grace

PROJECT KINGDOM COME

WOULD YOU LIKE TO ACCEPT JESUS INTO YOUR HEART?

THE BIBLE SAYS:

If you confess with your mouth that Jesus is Lord and believe in your heart that God has raised Him from the dead, you will be saved
(Romans 10:9)

SAY THE PRAYER BELOW OUT LOUD AND BELIEVE IT IN YOUR HEART!

Dear Lord Jesus,
I know that I am a sinner, and I ask for Your forgiveness.
I believe You died for my sins and rose from the dead.
I repent of my sins and invite You to come into my heart and life.
I want to trust and follow You as my Lord and Savior. Help me to live for you for the rest of my life.
I am now a child of God, and I ask You to fill me with Your Holy Spirit.

In Jesus' Name I pray, Amen.

Congratulations!
If you have prayed this prayer, please let an adult know or send an email to mybibleworkbooks@gmail.com

ANSWER KEY:

1.C
2.C
3.A
4.C
5.C
6.D
7.A
8.D
9.B
10. A
11. D
12. C

13.C
14.A
15.B
16.A
17.D
18.A
19.D
20.D
21.B
22. A
23. C
24. D

25.D
26.A
27.D
28.A
29.D
30.D
31.B
32.B
33.D
34.C
35.D
36.A

<<<<<< ANSWER KEY: >>>>>>

37.C
38.D
39.A
40.D
41.D
42.B
43.D
44.C
45.A
46.B
47.A
48.C

49.A
50.A
51.A
52.A
53.A
54.B
55.A
56.A
57.C
58.B
59.B
60.D

61.A
62.C
63.D
64.B
65.A
66.C
67.C
68.C
69.B
70.B
71.A
72.C

ANSWER KEY:

73. D
74. C
75. C
76. B
77. B
78. C
79. C
80. C
81. D
82. D
83. C
84. C

PLEASE GIVE US YOUR FEEDBACK!

Please send us your feedback on this workbook. We would love to hear what you enjoyed most, and ways you think it could be improved!

Please Send an email to: MyBibleWorkbooks@gmail.com, or leave us a comment on one of our social media pages.

 MyBibleWorkbooks@gmail.com

 Projectkingdomcome

 Projectkingdomcome

SCAN ME

And I am certain that God, who began the good work within you, will continue His work until it is finally finished on the day when Christ Jesus returns.

Philippians 1:6

DRAW HERE

DRAW HERE

DRAW HERE

DRAW HERE

DRAW HERE

www.ingramcontent.com/pod-product-compliance
Lightning Source LLC
LaVergne TN
LVHW060642110826
845147LV00018B/1022

9781961786042